The luck of a Caribbean does not exist

Nicole Sandoval

BookLeaf Publishing

India | USA | UK

Presentation by *BookLeaf Publishing*

Web: www.bookleafpub.com

E-mail: info@bookleafpub.com

ISBN: 9789360945237

First edition 2024

To my family:

You are all part of this journey.

Hope you are proud.

ACKNOWLEDGEMENT

My heart goes to everyone that had read me and encouraged me since I fell in love with writing. All of the friends that supported me through the learning process, all of the experiences lived and all of the sacrifices. Thank you for believing in me, inspiring me and being patient with me. Finally, I did it.

Special gratitude goes to my husband. Thank you for seeing me, believing in me, trusting me and giving me the opportunity to dream and create a home with you. Esta es por y para ustedes. Los amo!

PREFACE

Inspired by my daily life in the past 10 years, the book holds all kinds of feelings related to the reality of leaving absolutely everything behind and starting fresh in a new place. But this restart is in a setting where you don't feel connected, that you don't fit in, so it becomes a constant struggle for the re-definition of self.

These poems portray a very universal experience, and the idea is to insert your own experience within the emotion portrayed. There are no resolutions, just mysteries in the context of loss.

Airplane Mode

I used to be able to see the good and the bad.

The beauty and the chaos.
Differ from pure or evil souls.

I used to be able to switch at convenience
And use the visions in favor of my path.

I used to be proud of my extreme limits,
And made everyone around me find a bit to fit.

I used to be a lot of things.

But I am not.
Nothing.
Anymore.

I'm deep in the dark.
I see no light.
Not magic of any kind.

Unfortunately, airplane mode is set on
destruction.

Hell

The colors of the sea,
the formation of waves,
the smell of salt,
the taste of Island.

How can you be happy within your nature?
How can you feel in tune with the Caribbean
latitude where you are born?
How do you want to stay here?

The feeling is genuine.
The affinity is real.
The magic does exist,
and communicates with peace.

Palm trees guarding mountains.
How pretty your green is!
How delicious your air!
What height of spirit!
What a shitty government!

You have to let yourself die, let yourself be
trampled.
Let them steal our history and future.
All for the sake of survival.

Tuna or Anarchy

Looking out the window an invisible monster
watches me.
Silently digging through the agony.
There is no escape.
This is what his life is about.

He has been a custodian for years; never misses
a day.
His breathing intoxicates you, breaks your eyes
and irritates you.

Essential quality; necessary mark.
Attributes are accelerated by name.

Sugar misfortune; flavor disappearances.
All types of stopping.

Reciprocally imprisoning relationships.
Eternal centralization.

Let's paint pictures!
Now you do it.
Well done! Excellent.
"Puerto Rico rises!" (Mother fucker!)

Damn monster, you fog the nights of my
path—already dark and mysterious.
You infect my desire to be and stay.
Veins are impacted with burns.
The pen changes color, destiny, its objective,
correspondence, its place.

Distant waves.
Disproportionate repetitions.
To open doors you will find exits.
In half-opened windows there are no water slips.

The Ink Residence

I have never had a house.
I carry home with me.

The heat of silence.
The smell of loneliness.
The sound of the wind.
The vision of movement.
Self love.

Things come and go.
Places disappear.
The essence is permanent.

It's in the blood.
In the walk,
In breathing.
In the processing of situations.

I have never been friends with any door,
or window, or kitchen.

But I can remember the privacy,
the opportunity,
the food.
and the breath.

I choose books and words.
Chambers of other people's feelings.
I appropriate them.

Betting on holding the pen is faith and courage.
Or cowardice.
But it is the only future where I can reside.

Reflections of a Diaspora Indirectly Imposed by the Government

You swore fights.
Never to be afraid.
But you left.
You couldn't take any more shit.

The idea of a country is beautiful.
The magical corners.
Gifts from God.

You cannot eat divine wonders.
And even less on a capitalist island.
Where nothing belongs to us.
Much less politics.

The people are so conformed and ass kissers.
They don't think beyond rice and beans,
the garbage of the radio and the blind belief of
whichever church.

Ay bendito, but shut up, you can't give your
opinion!
You went away and left us.

From there, you can't fight.

Hatred and ignorance hide under the wing of the
supposed God.
While they kneel before the crumbs of the
colonizer.

Is there no capacity to open your eyes to the
immensity of the opportunity?

Writing is Serious Business

Deciding to be a poet in a hard and painful job.
Is lonely and dark.

Nothing like today:
Write today and publish tomorrow.
Then forget what I said.

They are not letters dead to oblivion.
They are not changing statuses with every
breath.
They are life itself in every breath.
They are the mornings full of hope for a
continuous future.

It's not a hobby.
It's not a plan B.
I repeat, it is not oblivion.

It is feeling the beats in blood and flesh.
It is the rhythm of destiny.
It is the sound of joy.
It is respect for peace.
It is the goodness of being in misery.

Being a poet is the acceptance of confinement.
Those expositions are just that, pure story.

Water Winds

1.
Return without returning.
We have to go back.
Those of us here are there.
Time to invest and down with the colony!
Let's build a country regardless.

I am an islander and ¿Qué pasó?
Water imprisons us instead of opening us to the
sea.
We need to explore new paths.

Who and what we are
We do not know.
We will find out on our way to justice.

2.
People do not necessarily live in their homes.
The place is relative.
We talk about the state with space.

Tuning is what is important,
Acceptance, belonging.

The moon in the window

the edge of the mountain,
Friends of the beach.

Tropical island.
From there. From here.
I'm leaving again.

I work for justice, recognition.
Prestige, value.
A better life.
Worthiness.
No corruption.

Everything is a process.
Natural and disciplined course.

The black ink routes are always the axis.
I always go back.
I can return.

How many notebooks have I filled?
It is time at the glance.
They are the transitions of life.
Gifting pens without houses and boxes of stray
things.

Homes are inside and not outside.
The exterior is the internal expression and
reflection.

3.
I went missing in the Caribbean.
It is known that poets get lost in time.
But the words are still there.
Of all. (Some so many fools).

What is destiny?
Who is God?
What are these things that happen?

It's hot!

The tropics.
Summer.
Still people without electricity.
The hurricane!
The society! Government!
The fucking weather!

I wait for the exit.
The transfer.
The job.
Discipline and passion.

Everything is aimed at the inner future.
Rest.

Peninsula Prayer

To: José Antonio Dávila and his sad love poems.

Creator of nature,
Maker of water-bearing lands
I want to make devotion, for the sadness of
simple things.

I transcribe a prayer
From the bottom of the afflicted chest,
With the hunger for the space that I carry in it
And with his thirst for return.

I don't have snow, but I am cold.
Loneliness stalks weariness.
The distance of being.

What was moved and lived.
It hurt.
The learned.

I need beach.
I need salt.
The suffocation of not being able to look.
The family warmth.
The skills that must be possessed when walking.

The prides,
The forgetfulness,
Which no longer matters.

The possibilities when returning.
The love of the already felt.

Great Creator,
Protect my miserable soul overwhelmed by
extremism.
Read and respond to my prayer of extension and
forgiveness.

-We are under Renovations-

15

Exile has made me unrecognizable.
Although I always maintain the fight and
education;
I have learned to be more patient.

Distance usually affects the focus of things.
And the structures do not shake enough to fall.
Will have to see.

Resentments

Social media.
Fashion,
Hair and body.

OMG! I'm so fucking cool.
Awesome photos.
Some shitty paints.
I must be an artist for sure.

Likes.
Hearts.
Questions and answers.
Pussy ass sucking.
Everything is fake.

Why fuck with intellectuals?
Why go into debt studying?
Experiences from privilege are the thing.
They are the true ones.
They are the aspiration.

Bitter, library rat,
Nobody is going to read you.
Just because you think you're a writer,
it means you are actually one.

Nobody reads your meaningless drivel.
One more, from the center of the universe,
which seeks the recognition of all evil.

You have to educate yourself, without a system
or university.
You have to criticize yourself, without similar
possibilities of understanding.
You have to laugh, before trying all the levels of
inequality.
You have to change the whole world, before
looking in the mirror.
You have to live without privacy, but with
coloniality.

Could it be that I also write without thinking,
so that I am able to walk.

In Five Shades

The sky in transparency.
The trees.
The light.

Is the time.
The traffic of life:
Planes
Birds
Insects and people.

Letters.
Home arrivals.
Cars.
Balconies.
Times.

Each of the five; from them.

From me.
From here.
Who will really know something?
There.

Some opportunities
are for taking them and assembling them.

Others to see them leave.

The sounds.
The alarms.
The songs of praise.

This is me in this, here.

When You Abandon a Literature Career

To Roberto Bolaño
When he wanted to write, he read the books and
lives of those now celebrated.
That in their respective presents they were
nothing more than souls in pain, surviving the
days.
The recipe was to observe and feel the days and
dedicate yourself to waiting.

But the trouble is that you suffer:
Being Caribbean without heat.
The distance from the golden beaches.
That a semi-voluntary exile is still real.
Government's shit is still true.

Meanwhile, it is needed to work on whatever
appears.
You have to fill your belly and contribute to the
account.

And again I find what made me fall in love with
life.
Not knowing that I am alone in the ink, awaiting
justice.

Transcribing and living compressed realities.

The hope is to be well judged.
Maybe even loved or studied.

The Luck of a Caribbean Does Not Exist

After years of strikes and struggles, we still have achieved nothing.
Our tropical future is very uncertain.
Living in paradise costs accepting waste and hell.

Resilience.
Endurance.

They are invoked in every breath of air,
As if we were proud of the abuses,
Of the insults and injustices of the empire.

God forbids to specify something.
Each one to do their own thing.
Homeland?
Who the fuck knows what that means?!?

Meanwhile, women die daily from cases of violence.
Elderly people and children suffer the pain of hunger and oblivion.
Ghosts of misery and corruption walk through our lives as owners and lords.

And there are those who believe they are very
untouchable.

"But, boy, shoot with everything; that we resist."
Taking our future in their hands.
The Caribbean bleeding into injustices.
Suffering unnecessary exile.

This, unfortunately, is the truth.

To the Rejected Island of the Caribbean and its Sands

From this cycle of sinking, what gets me out are the words.

What is mine is mine and nothing and no one can take it away from me. Not even the seven dusts of the Sahara.

Fuck hunger and hopelessness. Welcome to the pests.

Let everyone leave and not come back with false alarms.

Let them not shed their treasured tears.

May each of those empty lives explode in your souls.

The fight belongs to the strong, not the flamethrower.

Let those who can wait, smoking, for the return of the morning.

It is from the ashes that it rises and from the entrails it is that it is killed.

Sshhh! Move and shut up. I'm leaving and I don't know how soon I'll be back and then there won't be any more canned sausages.

I swear that sincere love waves in the wind. Education is and will be part of the alibi.

We don't want thanks. The sway and the gaze are enough for us.

To you, those lost by the stars of our wide universe, my close greeting.

Warmth inside.

To all of you, my place, the tropics.

Solve This Dilemma:

People like to give their opinions from their comfortable places and their movement radius of 25 miles, while others analyze from challenging spaces, with a radius of more than 1,227 miles.

Who will speak with greater perspective?

Humans are Shit

So much complication. For everything.

So many centuries of existence and we are still
not able to handle our existential, spatial
circumstances.

All Science. All Art. All God.

Complexity is perfection. Ah! Until it's different.
Because everything must be understood or
discarded.

To feel it or not to feel it.

Nothing escapes the rejection radius.

Hyper fragmented thoughts.

I swear that Universities* make us stupid. We
are still not able to stretch our thoughts without
some crutch of reference or validation.

What am I going to know about that one? I am
the one doing the thinking.

Between fear and hope. (I'm nostalgic).

– Could it be that I am doing something?

-Why do we have to do something?

-Well, to do something because we have to do something. About something.

-How the hell do you do something? Doing nothing is something.

-No. That's disrespectful.

-But if you stop you lose time.

-What are we talking about, what time?

-The one you really use to do something.

-Like what?

-Well, think. Without further ado. In everything. Just think.

I survive with water on my head.

With cookie recipes that I will never prepare.

I admire sweetness, but it's not for me.

-I seriously thought you were a humanist.

-I am.

-But your message...

-What's wrong with it? We aren't more because
we don't surpass ourselves. After so many
centuries, we still don't know how to think.

– It is sometimes called creating.

-Yeah. That is fine.

- If not?

– Falls in the rejection ratio. We don't stretch our
thoughts.

-#weareallpendejos

-#buttherearelevels

#wedidn'tunderstanddamnbutshesaysit'spoetry

-#goodforher

The happiness of imperfection. The shit of
writing.

Seeds that will germinate in time.

Light capacity.

Feel everything. Live with nothing.

Exist. Die.

* Also, the Churches. The leaders. All. To each
other

Suitable Habitat

32

On an island the sea encloses us.

Ah! But how free we are.

Dreams have wings.

And hope is eaten by scarcity.

Beauty lives in the corners,

While longing to sleep in family.

Going out where?

If outside, all that remains is to die!

Living in a Swamp

I miss the tropics.

I miss the weather.

Heat mixed with humidity.

The air with the sound of spirits.

The pleasant sensation of drowning.

The toast of the sun and the tanning of salt.

While flowers, birds and lizards surrounding
your house.

Mountains that rise and coasts that sink.

Pleasant prisons.

Caribbean wonders.

Nook Drawer

Most of my belongings are disposable.

Except for my books.

The rest lives in the memory.

Waves of the past that rumble on the shore of consciousness.

No regrets.

No forgiveness.

Remnants of pain and sacrifice.

Misunderstood secrets.

My materiality expires in seasons.

The rest waits on pages that may be colored.

Instagram Poetry

I live day by day,
from list to list.

A few of months,
others of years.

Like graffiti on the walls.
The lists move me.

Little by little, I'm moving forward.
The steps are getting completed.
Why is it so hard to see this?

Sometimes it feels like I'm doing nothing.
But I do, a lot.

This is how the path is being shaped:
Poetry, exercises, care for the kids, food, studies,
History, love and a little bit of forgiveness.

Relativities of Time

Light a cigarette as a reward.
Fight for liberty.
Present History.
Perform life.
Post a selfie.

Be awed with things that you encounter.
Enjoy beach hair and live the moments.

Concerts and dreams.
Early rise, movement and music.
Working hard, winning prices, doing art.
Getting high.
Drinking coffee.

Enter the winds and celebrate everything in life.

Conquer the world with banished eyes.
Wait for the weekend. Wait for the night.
Let's watch the sunset. Let's just vibe.
Let's declare love. Let's write.

All of this is absolutely necessary to survive.
Be everything and nothing. All at eleven.
So, we are able to keep on our path.

That is the only way my prayers become alive.
Withing heartbeats and breaths.
Letting unfortunate events be processed by the
sun.

Because gratitude is the only virtue that truly
gives sense to live.
There's nothing better than the experiences lived.
The challenges, the sacrifices, the breaking of
the soul.

Between moving and reading my life has
moved.
But my heart is always on an island bathed by
the Caribbean sun.
I can assure you that I always keep trying to
better myself, my day, my writing and the
people around me.

The future always bleeds. Hope resides in death.
With all the terrible, we still have life.

Suddenly, a tide of the past could push you with
all of its strength into the future.
Maybe, it could feel like you are drowning, but
it's actually saving your life.

www.ingramcontent.com/pod-product-compliance
Lightning Source LLC
LaVergne TN
LVHW010918200726
843509LV00013B/1982